THE AIR IN THE AIR BEHIND IT

"It is an ordinary, an orderly world offered to us in *The Air in the Air Behind It*, and yet this world surprises at every turn, and it throbs with mystifying energy. Every statement made threatens to dissolve into its opposite, every movement is a threat and a thrilling treat. The structure of most of these poems is of the sentence—while line breaks signal giddying turns, turns of phrase and fable both surprising and satisfying: 'Boredom makes me want/ to spill a secret to each bipedal/ organism passing/ on the street. I have a heavy heart. . .' and even this does not describe the compulsions of the book, or the way the language gets restrung like a glittery necklace broken with beads still lost under some of the furniture. Even up and down are unstrung, directions both comforting and treacherous: 'the sky called/ attention to the crater the people pointed/ and watched the comet from.' This is a book of consolations, open and inviting and yet as mysterious as fog, and as nurturing to a parched landscape."

—from the Judge's Citation by Bin Ramke

BRANDON RUSHTON was born and raised in Michigan. A recipient of awards from Gulf Coast and Ninth Letter, his poems appear widely in publications like *The Southern Review, Denver Quarterly, Pleiades, Bennington Review,* and *Passages North.* His essays have appeared in *Alaska Quarterly Review* and the critical anthology, *A Field Guide to the Poetry of Theodore Roethke.* After earning his MFA from the University of South Carolina, he joined the writing faculty at the College of Charleston. In the fall of 2020, he began as a Visiting Professor of Writing at Grand Valley State University in Grand Rapids, Michigan. With Josh English, he co-founded the poetry journal *Oxidant | Engine.*

THE AIR
IN THE AIR
BEHIND IT

POEMS

Brandon Rushton

TUPELO PRESS
2022

Library of Congress Catalog-in-Publication data available upon request.
ISBN-13: 978-1-946482-75-4

Cover and text design by adam b. bohannon.

First paperback edition September 2022

Tupelo Press
P.O. Box 1767
North Adams, Massachusetts 01247
(413) 664-9611 / Fax: (413) 664-9711
editor@tupelopress.org / www.tupelopress.org

Tupelo Press is an award-winning independent literary press that publishes fine fiction,
non-fiction, and poetry in books that are a joy to hold as well as read. Tupelo Press is
a registered 501(c)(3) nonprofit organization, and we rely on public support to carry
out our mission of publishing extraordinary work that may be outside the realm of the
large commercial publishers. Financial donations are welcome and are tax deductible.

For Mom, Dad, and Mara

CONTENTS

And wherever two currents meet, especially if they differ sharply in temperature or salinity, there are zones of great turbulence and unrest

RACHEL CARSON

THE AIR IN THE AIR BEHIND IT

Milankovitch Cycles

> We as a species are lessened by the loss
> of unknown places.
>
> PAULINE DROBNEY

In an age of emergency, experiments are always the first things to be abandoned. It happens gradually or so the glaciologists agree. Something massive moves in, melts, and rapidly meanders out. A lone mammal dips its nose in the river. Leave it to something celestial to abbreviate nomadic momentum. A meteor cuts through the low cloud-cover and all the stampeding herds abruptly stop and stand bewildered. Parents call the kids from their kitchens, but the kids are on their backs in the black night, on the black grass, with the light of the already-over leading near. Inside, televisions

tout a sports story: a front runner is swallowed by the pack that's been pursuing now, for laps. Commentators ramble relentlessly into the evening about endurance, how nice it must be to go on like that forever, to be as infinitely lucky as a light year seems. Legend has it

the sail is a product of the Stone Age. The waves and the ancient wonderers about to see whether they're seaworthy. The rest is history. A conquistador steps off a ship in a new world and loses his stomach on the shore. Getting a good look at his insides a shop owner pulls his mangled hand from a meat grinder. The small mistake a butcher makes in the busy hour. The city bustles by and not a note is taken in the bustling.

Not about the pocket-money raining on the pedestrians from the person dangling from the balcony above. Not about the driver pulling her lover's face back through the windshield. Violence

finds a way. The meteorologist agrees there is a great momentum. History happens in waves, nomadic hunters hefting spears that—in their arching—turn into arrows, turn into cannonballs, turn into bullets, always more efficiently turning the target's insides out. Extinction is a byproduct

of evolution. The global grid goes down and the earth seems quite deliberate in its darkness. Mass graves are continual signs of our malfunction. Breath clouds crowd the square as the convicted traitor is shot at nightfall in the snow. A photographer takes pictures of an unpopular regime, buries the photographs in jars after everyone agrees democracy is a better way to dictate terms. War is, first and foremost, a mimicry of the geological processes of the planet it is fought upon. A convergent boundary. A collision of forces in a confined space. Plates collide and mountains sprout from all the crashing, jagged and monstrous with snow collecting at the caps. This is the place where clouds obscure the colder weather and its wandering, where all the good sled dogs go to die. None of this explains the strange

phenomena, the forest opening up to absorb the airplane. The tall trees where the skeleton of the hang glider holds on. It's not the story that's important, but who they sell it to. A little bird of an early settler leaves the settler's shoulder and beelines down the canyon. He called for it once and then kept calling. The main objective is finding the difference between what had to go and what has gone. The landowners lease off what's left of their anemic acreage. It's common knowledge: the West was won one weed killer at a time. When the people can't make sense they manufacture myth. They talk about the future like the unfolding events won't take them there. Even the earth is elliptical, affected

by the gravitational pull of other planets. No wonder the adolescents tilt their magnifying glass to engulf the parading ants. Everything moves one way or the other. The cartographers won't stop talking about adaptable careers—how they charted and, now, charter. The bus lets everybody off to flashbulb the blitzed and blinking landscape. A railroad comes and goes. The buffalo roam in a diary of a dirty prospector who died a hundred years ago today. It's important to bury embarrassments. For example

in the wee hours the least talented talk show host takes the reins. The cable company calls back all its vans. All the antennas begin to spin like weathervanes. Directionless, the broken vase makes the lovers sing the baby back to sleep. Hushed tones and howling in the hand-me-down suburban home. A nomadic hunter picks up a pinch of sand

and lets it loose, points his party toward the over-there, the yonder plains, the uncontainable continuum of years. Revolution means this all comes back around: ice sheets carving up then carving out a way, the turbine towns siphoning the wind, the little lightning fires burning what they may then burning out.

What if There's Something Out There

Like clockwork everybody calls for their kids
to bring the kites in. Turns out, the street
is as much of a drag as we thought it'd be.
Lately, everyone I look at looks a lot alike.
They're all searching for a word to wind me
down. I say hi to a man that looks like history
and then I have to hear about the stretch
of years he's had. A man my dad would call
old dog, but do so lovingly. I don't know
anything anymore about endearment. Not a
lick about how any of this is meant to end.
For example, the inspector says the gas leak
should have done us in. I start to believe
in things I've never seen before. Like Utah,
or fate. It's a big sky. When the celestial
passes close everybody will stop and want
to be the comet. Maybe then the type
of mattress finally won't matter. Maybe then
not even the vague notion the neighbor holds
about our oven lamp. Just because
it's internal doesn't mean the light wont leak.
All of us in our parkas on the lawn. All of us
walking around like we have some story
someone someday is going to care enough
to collect. The film ends, the teacher flips
the switch, and everyone just closes their eyes.

The New Century Springboard

It always has something to do
with the debatably corrupt attention
we must pay to arithmetic

and time. A rheumatologist says
reflection is a lesson the clock
can't teach us, so she invites her younger

patients toward a pond,
a puddle, a larger lake to see
their stares returned by someone

who looks refracted, but alike. The light
sure looks older than
it is. The days are slow and filled

with supermarket sales.
A rock thrown through a tree house
window wakes the sleeping

people in their homes along
a residential street. A yapping dog
settles down inside the yard a car

cuts its engine at the edge of—
to question a guilty-looking group
of boys who insist they did not

spend their morning in the woods.
　　　　Make what you will
of the weather, of the ball game banter

　　　　of bored folks fantasizing
about the billiard table, lonesome
　　　　and lacking players

at the bar. The planning committee
　　　　commissions an artist
intending to increase the desirability

　　　　of town. Tour buses never come,
neither do the dollars. Therefore,
　　　　the community they have for so long

been deliberating, winds up sub-divided.
　　　　Sawmills sell the lumber
for fences folks intend to lean on

　　　　while peeking at the neighbors
looking stiff, stretched out there
　　　　on their lawn chairs eating lunch.

Despite the poor excuse for an exercise
　　　　space, public pools
offer plenty for children in their time

　　　　of play, who dare each other
on the diving board above
　　　　the one they jumped from

just before. Through the shade
       of his sunglasses, a podiatrist
suggests they better watch

       their step, which the children take
to mean: *don't get caught doing the wrong*
       thing very long. How unlikely

it is anymore to lead by example, or
       in that fashion
learn. Jet contrails expand then pull apart

       conspiracies about the poisons
they contain. Atmosphere looks like
       atmosphere again. Real estate

appears as artificial as the lawn
       one waters while the kids keep
looking up toward the planes. Rubbish

       is what the rich people call
the wreckage left in the wake
       of all the rockets. They watch

for a bit and then feel bad about
       the broadcast up until it's time
for bed. On her way home, a hard worker

       runs the car through a stop
sign, near-missing a cyclist, and hitting
       a hydrant as the broken pipes

pump water higher and higher into
            the night. A young girl puts her
finger back inside her pocket, deciding

            it's better if she doesn't point.
Family members joined at a dinner table
            bless the food, made

of chemicals bound to break their bodies
            down. The adults gather in a den
and shake together something stiff

            to ease the tension in the joints
beneath their skin. Upstairs, the kids
            push their beds in front of a door

and say bad words to each other
            in the dark. Everyone collapses
here and there—in the car, in the chair, or

            on the couch without asking
what they've done or if they did enough
            today to deserve it.

Alternative Terms for Tomorrow

In this age all other age becomes the briars
the kids kickstand their bikes beside both
cars the parents bought in an effort to
permanent their love the landscape painters
vow to capture the look of the lock the ships
slip through at dusk in summer the students
shortchange the sherbet trucks and run
the block the apartment buildings duplicated
and drawn out of their hives the bees barely
festering in the air away from the regulars
a man orders two Diet Cokes and switches
personalities each time he takes a drink
two parents face the sad reality that they are
trying to remember when they weren't
looking the kids came home with someone
else's house cat on a leash which led them
to believe they could be born again at sunrise
the recreational lovers are rug burned and out
of breath the delivery boy stares a long time
at the dirt his boots brought in from the wild
mind the milkshake maker has a theory what
if the buses take them far apart and continue to
the coast and then the beach with some sad
wrappers wrangled in the reeds the evidence
of a slim gap between a gullet and a garbage
chute confirms the way to waste such wonder
is to watch it in this age all other age becomes
the maniacal eyes at the edge of the field
they made themselves believe were lighting bugs

A Rhombus

The bus in this city
smells and sounds just like a bus
in every other city

and so the young boy
on the street stops
to ask what haven't we

homogenized. Hardly
able to distinguish between
her own house and the next

door neighbor's, a dentist pulls
into a driveway and expects
the kids who are not hers

to lend a hand. The stairwell
to our walkup is wet and full
of lettuce, meaning

the old man has dropped
his groceries once again.
In an hour and a half it will be noon.

By then the breaking news
of bombs buckling a building
broadcasted on everybody's

screen. *It's all happening*, says the pilot
        to the rising sun, just before
her plane disappears without a blip

        or bleep from sea. Finding
what looks to be a fossil, a beach goer
        holds up his bounty

toward the light. And isn't it just
        like light to fill
an empty space. Here and gone

        and just enough dust
to assume some trace. Just outside
        the park is a path where

healthy people like to jog. A dog
        here and there dividing
the trail diagonally. A young girl

        drops her bag beside
the door and says shapes are what
        she learned in school

today. Two parallel lines
        will never meet. A block
is formed by four separately

        named streets. Triangles
are geographic shapes geographers
        avoid for fear

of vanishing. An arm interrupts
      a distracted ambler
from the crosswalk just in time

      to pull him back
from the rim of something elemental.
      Indivisibility is hard

is all the people heard, walking away
      from the scene, divided.
Lampposts suggest, at some point,

      the light runs out. Mothers
call for their sons. A group of boys
      in a garage scrapping

the bike they stole from another
      boy the day before.
Each night is another night without

      a ransom note. What a bummer
that must be. In an effort to maintain
      a heightened sense

of mysteriousness, the mailman
      phones himself
from an unknown number. The moon

      does that funny thing
where everyone looks young again
      like you'd remember

them. What was real once can't be
　　　　　real forever. Everyday we wish
to go to bed a little better. Then

　　　　　the power plant
magnetizes all our sleep. The road
　　　　　is wide open and the sudden

stone chip in the windshield
　　　　　makes us cry. A phone rings
and the people in the pool

　　　　　start whispering. Someone
to say the street looks dark
　　　　　and welcoming. Someone

who calls to ask what shape
　　　　　I'm in and why.

No Known Natural Predators

Let's say—for the first time—something new
becomes the focus of the suburban centerfold.
A backyard brochure that finally embodies
the complacency of the community taking so much
pride in welcoming—with what they say–
is open arms. The young boy has his doubts, it seems
about the dare, and insists upon a rope
around his waist before he'll run out across that thin-
and-freezing-thicker pond. Anything lost will agree
there is a distance you can't be dragged back from.
I sit in a splintering wooden chair by the window
and it all sounds more like nervousness than new.
To the slow surprise of every patron, the place
becomes a figure of what cannot continue on. Perpetuity
is a target the powerful throw their darts at.
Let's be honest, who wouldn't want to linger
a little longer than allowed. There is a point
at which the pop-up vendors will say enough is enough
and make their market somewhere else. Perhaps
transaction is only the tone we take with each other
when it's only us talking. Like before any form
of light, in the early morning, when the grass is wet
and we—with little purpose—welcome
whatever residue that leisurely appears. We want things
to stick around. We keep forgetting it isn't
our invitation to extend. Our matters are microscopically
small considering a widower on a highway west
of here faces the idea that his lover is, now, just particles
his headlights pass through. After dinner, an analyst
steps out into the cold and attempts to breakdown

the sad part of a breath cloud. Barely legible
is the handwritten note, rain-stained and lucidly sarcastic
under the windshield wiper. *The community
has decided the street is not—and will never be—a public
parking lot.* Peeking out from a huddle of covers
are the children. The place is cozy. All of the neighborhood
parents speak peacefully knowing there is a line
dividing their properties. Their illegal on-goings go down
in a fluorescent orange motel on the edge of town.
Innocent isn't the word I'd use. Overall, we are a people
made up mainly of an abnormal amount
of moon landings. Make no mistake, all additional assets
are monitored and secure. All that has been refined—
in this age—is our collective efforts to rest assured.
Kicking her feet back, the Forest Service Officer
watches the smoke-wall widening, emulating the incessant
impulse of the woods. There's nothing else to do.
The fire burns excessive acreage, a local bar, but spares
the cabin with the cut grass. This is how chaos convinces
the passive to come to terms, an accidental acknowledgement
of fate. The same way an open pasture promises enough
to make a motorist pull over. The motorist with his hands
in his pockets, breathing slow. The motorist whose car
explodes behind him—on the side of the expressway—in the rain.
Who can blame the way—in its quiet elongation—time pauses
just a little bit so the people driving by can form a picture
in their minds—of a car exploding, on the side
of the expressway, in the rain. Everything becomes, and then
belongs to the invisible register of stories. Something
to break the silence, something—in the half-lit dusk—to tell
a person you are not totally in love with. I saw once
an apathetic shopper shudder at a product that promised

it was shatterproof and—by doing so—removed themself
from apathy. With a rope around his waist, the young boy runs
wildly out across the ice. Through his act, it is apparent
the community understands there is a choice: to be dismantled
or to disappear. No one cuts the rope. No one has enough
guts to do the good thing. A crowd gathers in a courtyard to hear
a speaker give a speech that sounds revolutionary
but is quite unclear. A boat captain coughs into her hands
and watches the town grow dim from her ship, offshore.
Trees tip up and tell us from which way to expect the weather.
Everything is a little off-kilter. For example, the blindfold
on the mannequin the paparazzi use for target practice.
Tabloids hardly ever handle heartbreak, gracefully.
Picture this: a cinema ticket-taker wrestling with the complex
mechanics of making a moment last longer
than it should. It is so appropriately us, sizing up an abandoned
house from the street, deciding whether or not
to credit card the door lock and take a look around. A tire
and a truck topper in the yard, laundry left out
on a clothesline to deter all would-be bandits, but—already worn
by multiple winters—we see it unraveling: the concept
of crafting an appearance of a timely coming home.

Before the Experts Mislabeled the Beyond

There's so much they could have done
for each other and a lot they could have
generally just done. It was summer
so evening came differently to the kids
on the wet roofs dreaming of cosmonauts.
Down the road, teens packing the truck
for a camping trip were told to be careful—
since people do disappear and occasionally
wake up in a cabin in the woods with a hole
in their side where a kidney was. Like always
the forecast called for fog, a slow commute,
an unknowable future. The lead story led off
with a kind of fear that could keep two people
in love from becoming parents: a newborn
snatched from a backseat of a station wagon
in Wyoming. Plucked, it seemed, straight
from the indiscernible blur of the blue above,
the open air through which everything passes
as preventable in retrospect. Nothing goes back
to the way it was before. Before the experts
mislabeled the beyond they just called it *out
there*. Before the other tourists realized
the screaming couple lost their child
they just called them *out there*. Time is as
hysterical as each event the people promised
to process down the road but did not
return to. The stars flashed forward and found
them there, the kids, alright, and saying they were
alright with a long drive to the coast, what was
left of it, the warped boards the weather broke

where years ago a young boy washed out
with the waves. They ran through sand
and sounds of shore birds in the breeze
and disregarded the way the water came up
farther than before, the boy it once washed
away, how *out there* tenses seemed rudimentarily
unfit, how they ignored the historical plaque
that said whoever had been holding his hand
let go of it.

Sound Barrier

Science is fundamental
to my misunderstanding, you must
know. Beam fastened

into beam and then a building
growing taller by the day.
I ask earnestly for what sake

.   other than the sake
of speed. To breach or bypass
like a bridge over the river

running now, below. I hold up
my hand to block the sun
and partake in the partial obfuscation

of the self. A shadow casted
out a window wants back in. The sewer
grate cannot re-inhale

its steam. The people go on being
people who would rather
otherwise ignore. A monument

overtakes the public square,
the flowers there, the trees the people
tie their hammocks to.

Swaying little, like ethical implications
          of diminishing the wind,
the wind the neighbor wakes up

          and secures her screen
against, a weather-front moves in
          and creates very little change.

Except for the construction crane
          pointing in a direction a little
different than it did the night before.

          A bath from up above seeps
through our ceiling fan and fills another
          pail. We pour it down the drain,

standing at the sink to stare. Funneling
          financial advice could scandalize
the stories a future magnate might try

          to sell. Out of the core
of common curiosity and the depths
          of fudged data, allegations

sweep through the higher court
          and are swiftly covered
up. What better an arrangement

          than the bed I fall face into
after fighting through the day.
          If you don't mind I'd like to rest

a moment, though *there's no time*
        like the present feels a lot like a
misrepresentation of my precious absence.

        I should be gone or studying
concepts of sleight of hand, but instead
        I fall asleep with my face against

the seat ahead of me. This is how it feels
        right now and how I almost thought
it'd feel forever. I stand a moment in the light

        of a gas station I'm generally
just fond of. I feel tiny against the backdrop
        of the traffic. And to that tininess

I tip my hat, I smell the bus only after
        it blows past me. I am known or
unknown always because of noise.

        As the no-cause-for-alarm I am
I try to tiptoe through the apartment
        using only cell phone light and

stub my toes. Traffic screeches to a halt.
        Buildings outlive the people
who populate, repopulate, and make it

        a point to persistently pass through.
The land splits open and the street
        of cars slides single-filed, straight in.

I come dangerously close to some
        partition, some fog I can't stop
my want to fit inside. In a rush

        of mountainous air I mistake me
for myself again. To have been crossed
        and then crossed so many times

you lose your edge. This place that hardly
        now exists. I take a photograph
to memorialize the view. I shake it still.

        It is the shaking not the stillness
that persists.

These Proliferations

I was aware of movement around me, my fellow beings

driven by a mindless fetish for action —

LOUISE GLÜCK

It can't but probably all is nonsense. The newsmakers exactly

unremarkable inside it and around. The construction sites

ratcheting up up and out of their own way of. In the heat

the humans have a handle on, some clouds a helicopter chops

through, close at first and then up and down the coast.

The morning and it broadly gesturing at all that's good. The beach-

group out from under it becoming observant of the fact

they never were. A dam upriver lets some water down. The day-

jobbers juke through traffic to and fro. Some water passes

people pausing for a train and the day unfolds like the talk

they stumble into. Light goes briefly on above the garages,

in the lots, and on the leaves that make a gutter grow.

Wind makes first the weather move and then the wonder

of the family in the window watching out. Water gathers

in the streets the drivers arriving, finally, and dutifully informed

about the storm they had to readjust their routes around.

It's a town beside a town that looks exactly like the others.

Things then happen that none of them thought up. They recognize

the rules, the laws, the logic upon which they barely base

themselves. Across a tabletop a theory stretched a focal point

covered by a finger that put it on the map. An apparition rises

that'll years from now realize how wrong the time was to rightly

say their happiness was lost. A pigeon and a plot point on the patio

the rain puts out the cigarettes before they're smoked. Buildings

crumbling and birds making nests from that debris, though

they (them) do not derive a single knowledge nor acknowledge

any ever being so. The bridge becomes so many. The engineers stay

busy blueprinting up a grid for going off of. For them, the measure

of the dream was that they had it. It's all a breath the ball players toss up and bat away. Where individually the people go goes away

together what gathering they might have been. They step off

the bus into a day they'd planned to miss. Someone said they saw

how others felt and saw. Someone said they'd built some space

for themselves and that was all.

Puddle Jumper

Brought up by the bay made the boy about
the water or the rocks or a bridge between
the boroughs sad people often stroll
and sneeze into their handkerchiefs the pollen
collecting in the air vents of the vehicles like
fuzz the sun stuck across the cars on the top
deck of the parking garage a grudge a guy
took out on tires makes the people talk
across their patios from which the kids
planned to shoot the pigeons either way

Vertically the rappellers robbed the bank vault
and rendezvoused in a diner clinking mugs
one pastor paid another for the pills
the waiter knew his mother needed
to face the fact there was not about to be a bus
of people and plastic grocery bags at dawn
the sun coming in through the office windows
and the lovers mistakably still in one another's
arms the scene was argumentatively not rural
although after the tornado the stairwell climbed
up into nothing but the sky

Perhaps the private life is on the public train
the pond fog splits around the neighborhood
the weather eroding patio chairs and pages
from a perfume magazine strewn all along
the bike path in the early morning a kid climbs
down from a tree house and hustles home
to send a message a good friend simply gives
a glance the grocery shopper carries with her
through the day a meal she decided on
just then the power from the fuse box circuits
out and the kid walks in on his elders to explain

From behind the cloudbank the plane
reappears at the pharmacy the pill capsules
full of pencil shavings improperly employed
the balloon pilot busts through the roof
of the arboretum on his back a blue boy
looks up at a blue sky and says blue things
below the engine in the air above the water
the pilot thinks about the waves pushing
up against the boat in a place she used to be
aware of the hours slipping away from home
she stopped herself at the closet but left
everything but the year books in the back

The jacket draped across her knees blocks out
the cold way she packs a cooler for the mountain
climbers they circled back for that were bones
by the time they got there the sun was setting
and the sea was calm so she cursed the bike she
borrowed to pedal to a cliff to point out porpoises
bloated on the shore the tourists take some time
to bathe in the day's last light and a moth dizzies
over with a letter in its mouth and she reads it
while everything around her waits

Public Works

Dismissed from some other duty
the drawbridge attendant questions
the stability of days. As in: how long
until what we've been holding on to
finally gives way. A paycheck comes
and the only thing we find puzzling
is its amount. *Hold up*, yells a stranger
and we breathe easier when we know
he's talking to the bus. We're all in this
together. The commute. The tailpipes
we press our tonsils to. Figuratively
we see ourselves in the frozen lake,
the one we drive by coming back
from lunch. Looking out pessimistically
a shoe polisher prepares to be replaced
and counts his years. Everybody has
an idea about real work: it is digging
down to and replacing the seepage
bed. It is dirty and always thankless.
New ideas come and go while we wonder
which of those they might permit.
A municipality complicates the matter
with a makeshift levy. Taxes that
which cannot take another hit.
A vendor on the street takes down
her sign. The roof we nail-gunned
together, collapses in. How marvelously
one explosive in a lunchbox can light up
a square. For the sake of national security
we're asked to get some sleep. Daybreak

can only represent the way we rise

and shatter. We'll all be getting up soon.

Like all of us, you are so much, right now

just snow. You scrape the ice

from the windshield, check the handle

of each door, and swear: *this is not the way*

I'll be worn down.

The Waylayer

Heard it first from the foreman
the frost outside
the windows the factory
the smoke stacks rising up and out of
earshot of the shore
the joggers joking briefly
here and there
then on a bench
above the dam
by the water they'd find the body in
states of undress and disarray
so confounding
were the angles
of the light like remembering
the burnt taste the coffee had
that cold morning by the lake
the lovers lost something notable
in the distance
no one sure exactly what
it meant to them
it meant so much
frantic searching for
a lead the cops combed through
the welcome ledger
the warehouse workers kept
a detailed list of drivers
and delivery trucks
in a desk drawer
the plant manager hid a pistol
and a pipe for incidents like that

the hired hand carried out
the evidence
in unassuming stacks
of folders the forensic team
paid no attention to
as they were rushing in
a crowd slowed
discreetly in the street
to form a kind
of meaning meant to counteract
the man on the corner calling
for the end occasionally
a lonely lover drives toward
the cliffs abruptly cold
and suddenly with few
convertibles with tops drawn back
along the coast
the beach houses
boarded up and weeds and reeds asleep
along the roundabout
the lights appearing
in the homes of people
headed off to assemble parts
of the story are withheld
of course the foghorn
in the distance
like an inexact anxiety or ache
around a joint the job
wore down the decades
into dust their duties
changing over time
they'll tell you

they're older than
they never planned
to be a landmark
or a namesake
for the bridge
they grow quiet about
remembering the man
who stood on its handrail
with all the unknown
details the townsfolk
hammered after
work they walk it still
and talk about it now
the cold the boats the sound
his body made when it hit
the harbor ice below

All Night After Erasing the Equations

The scientists come back after the bad
experiment and debate the explanation
they'll report to their superiors. Probably
the plan just wasn't meant to be.
The pilots cut the engine in the middle
of a crucial maneuver and were distracted
by the moon. The people on the launch
pads were impressed. Shielding the kids'
eyes with one hand and the kids' pulling
those hands away with their own, it became
clear all were drawn toward what explodes.
Like most senators, those conducting
the follow-up hearing failed miserably
at throwing fits. The scientists were not
surprised. Of course a stunt like theirs
would get their funding cut. The reporters
asked—to no one in particular—who among
them, there, wasn't some deranged animal
or a Midwestern dad that, for luck,
carved his daughter's name into his cue stick
so the angle of his debts might be solved.
They had a point, but it faded before
they finished making it. Perhaps, the committee
said, there is no reason to believe the scientists
have purged themselves of the politicians
inside them. The people lost interest
in public life and how things were.
They just wanted to know if happiness
was there; that the shopping carts would

still have a place for the kids; that the good
animals weren't used for glue; that if the timing
was right, they could still take the heart
out of one person and put it in another.

Roll Call

Probably practicality is just going to bed

with a glass bottle on the door handle
for so many years. We have the right

to be alarmed. I grow considerably

skeptical of the automation
conditioning my air, the way

the geologist forgoes his vocation

and studies only the goose bumps
on the body lying quietly

beside him. On his behalf I'll say—considering

the corrosive wind—the cliffs
are appropriately anemic. Cataloguing

every lost cause, the climber convinces

himself he is not to blame. This is how
thin the air gets on the high road

how mist becomes a euphemism

for a memory I can't wrap
my mind around. Light leaks in through

a window in the morning and suddenly

your young frustrated daughter
is in the doorway asking what your life

was like before her living. I have such a very

hard time comprehending
the course of history before

my having been, and take at least

some small relief, in the fact
that all the fields are oblivious

to the amount of books that note

the battles fought upon them. A guest
lecturer excuses herself and reemerges

through the double doors

but this time in disguise. A lapse of time passes
in anticipation because anticipation

is one long, ecstatic pause. The way that people

calling timber hold their breath up until
the conclusion of the toppling. Are the trees here?

The dendrologist wants to know

if the trees are here and if she can expect
we've accepted they assist us

in our living. We are all constantly pursuing

a feeling until the feeling we had once
was felt again. The attendant admits

when she's on a quest to change

her chemistry she crushes
another pill, grows frustrated

that the receipt roll is always on the verge

of running out. Pink smears across
everything, including the highway

and the tires as the traffic passes. Headlights

shine out from the edge of cliffs toward
the history and cargo that constantly

washes up against the walls. Kids find

a wardrobe from the last century and lope
like socialites along the shore, collecting shells

and stones to situate neatly next to the glasses

of some gone and buried grandparent gathering
dust in a drawer upstairs. It's like the old days

haven't disappeared a bit, instead they fill

the room around us. In an effort to adopt
the latest fashion we purchase a section

of shag carpet and call ourselves

bohemian. For better or worse the cyclical
nature of the news makes the population

nauseous. Recent events prove nothing

except an overwhelming capacity to please
pundits, who incessantly carry on about

an impending agrarian resurgence. A recreational

cyclist rides so far into the farmland he mistakes it
for the future. Time is a little satchel full

of seeds, an activist who planted a plot of saplings

and returns each year half suspecting
to find they haven't grown. We look out upon a place

until the place asks us to excuse

its absence. Shadows in the distance do things
like they should be done. They dodge

the guard dogs, expose a hole

in the fence, slip through, turn around, and together
make it wider. An air balloon rises and rips

a cloud during the course

of its ascension. Nothing worth noting happens
normally. It's no surprise. I didn't wake up

in a new place to feel like the same old person.

The Dark Horse Accompanies a Friend
Away from Pentecost Camp

The mattress made it hard to sleep
so they sat up picking apart the wallpaper
whispering beside the water the boards
on the barrel-dock creak back and forth
like what's left of the crickets
and the season that summoned them
in the mulch pile by the shed the millipedes
make waste among the woodchips
with their mouths the two girls unable
to discern their beginning from their end
of the road the route looked less wooded
looking back the two of them noticed
no lamp no light in the dark windows
of the bunkhouse they left behind oblivious
to the bold gestures the bats make
for the bugs around them in the air
were subtle hints and hues for example
the color of the crops and the bite
the breeze had as the grown-ups gathered
them in gowns all the girls agreed
they wanted nothing to do with the future
their rolled back eyes revealed
the blurred fur beneath the bird feeder
in the fog of years good friends disappear
into an existence only they know
now the twisted promises of tongues
and touching in the reeds the river
the pastor dips the people in
to prop them up redeemed

the congregation grows and gathers
in the barn the girls break at in the dark
the hay like the hair they run their hands
through by the road the geese going
somewhere in the sky above the highway
growing black and at the real probability
of going back they flail their hands
they wave they flag down a tired truck
driver who shakes his head and caves
at the kids' request and honks

The Far Away Farm

        Haven't been. Not lately
at least the lover I was born
        to be. Some hopscotch

stone suspended in its toss
        and the world around it
waiting patiently. Time resumes

        its pace and patterns
on the street, like everything
        decay. I think of those

who came to visit me and what
        the days were like the days
they did. The season smelled

        like orchard work and you
in a dress time won't allow me
        to describe. We cannot leave

it as it is, it seems. The room
        aroma-less and warm, or
rearranged as we require space

        for new appliances. A stove,
an ottoman pushed in and guests
        disappointed that our things

appear exactly as they are and never

        change. Certainly the paneling

is capable of age. As are the people

        who inside it host a private

gathering. Surely, it should be

        categorized as that: an affair

which was not our own, but

        the property of many. They have

come this far to find us out, we're sure

        of it. We do well except when in

my wild excitement I mispronounce

        a mountain range. The party

promptly coming to a halt. You

        having half expected it

look for the closest out. Then on

        cue a car horn honks

and all attendees turn attention

        to the street. All that was not

acknowledged then is now

        a mystery. Moreover

an aroma. An afterglow from what

        appeared to be a gathering

of friends. Now: a heavily sedated sky

        we keep our secrets

in. You slipping out upon the patio
             to say *yes* that is the sun
that's peeking and perhaps my lack

             of sleep won't keep me
from my work on time. Which isn't
             much, of course. Just me

making my way without anybody
             taking note. Not really
morning yet and it surely isn't

             night. Cars still parked
and cloud patterns passing over
             them, streetlights

obscured nearly by the fog, people
             disappearing into it and me
stopping to say something

             to the dog. You must have
felt it too, I'd guess. The gust
             that slapped the street

of open windows shut. It isn't a new
             thing to assume time
has trouble keeping up. It lengthens

             and then retracts. The morning
reporter looking sad when things
             are shot and wrapped. I see you

waving from the bridge, hoping
        I've returned with bagels. Maybe
I've misunderstood the warp, maybe

        you the weather we are
under. A truck passes close
        chock-full of barrels. A tin can

the kids kick down the road. Wherever
        they go they go there rattling
and return unrecognizable next summer.

Story They Told You They'd Tell You in Time

Everyone was meeting
at the lodge allegedly
to discuss the lake
receding having just
revealed the tractors
the token rust
dumped and beaten up
the good dad with bad habits
perpetually calls home
and hands them down
the road the river the creek
the bundled children promised
to come back from by now
a woman swears
she should have seen them
the blue oceans the better country
but braids her daughter's hair
instead of her lips or lap
against the face of her lover
a detective stares deep
into the dilated dark
pupils of the truck stop prostitutes
and it is late where they are
and full of lights
the flatbeds freight toward
and then away
from the evidence the suspects
acquiesce they cough up
they decide to come clean
about the corpse

the housekeeper found
was their friend
whose arm they said
they left the needle in
when the knocking started
they said they believed
it was a bust they believed
they had to bust it
they said so they said
believe us everyone
on the motel bed felt bad
about the weather brewing
from afar and in it
the boaters broke for home
and this is how it was
that lonesome felt farther
and farther away the boat
the outboard motor on the back
the wake splits behind
and then apart a lot like leaving
someone standing on the land
reminds the markers
of the distances
between two storms
you were born
on a pallet in a barn
while outside the thunder
made the horses go berserk
the fence blitzed
and broken down
you rode in on a thing
none of us could name

that feeling the fog
in the trees beside the farm the fields
the detective looking off toward
the road the grass beside it
bending easy and without fuss
it feels like something terrible
she says it feels like the space
the air makes for the flatbeds
passing through she came
to name it what we call it now
this wild this fugitive wind

The Ladderless

Every other alchemist awake in the witching
hour understands how cold the corpses are in
the cabin the avalanche has covered so many
acres the airplane continues its reconnaissance
above the reservoir because it doesn't know
the war is over and the welcome home
is a light rapping at the door and a domestic
scene inside the crockpot is a slow cooked
batch of curses for which they say she should
be stoned so she gets stoned and sleeps soundly
with a shotgun in her lap reclining in the chair

After the runaways have smeared their faces
with plant resin and rendezvous in an abandoned
rail car the faces over the floorboard fire conjure
all kinds of stories of faulty farm equipment
and the causalities they caused a deep divide
the trail between the cabin and the boathouse
will always fork and end with two kids at summer
camp in love agreeing they have such a long time
together a bank teller and a liquor store cashier
decide the dream is not rising and dressing as
they've done enough already they leave to oversee
a compound in a county uninhabited up north

It would be unbecoming of the polar explorers
not to press on into the upper territories
of the wild head she's had for years she says
the forecast has fuzzed over and frosted out
of the tree line stutters some pastor tripping
on pentobarbital the ice artists only stop
to sculpt the igloos in their minds and what
brochure advertises a sight this morning refusing
to be seen between the sacrilegious fog that skirts
the tree stumps and the tired saw gives away
a greed the hedges had she remembers the bend
in the road but not the church in a field behind it

It is when the lease on the land runs out they learn
the heart is made up of so many acres the forager
drops the task at hand and decides to do something
different for a spell the levitation one seems weaker
than when it was first taught to her the fire burned
down and then the frost on the bed the blankets
covered something still the morning must reveal
the rustic barn and beside the road toward it a pail
of water ported halfway home and then abandoned
there you have it the field and the flowers the fence
posts steady was her hand when the wind was
precisely the song she swore her missing sister sung

The decrepit shape of the rafters governed their going
farther in and around it what had fallen and flapped
about the weather the wind had other plans potentially
everyone in the foyer anticipates a kettle at least a range
of land to look out at and the light stretching on
over their heads the dreams that helicopters might
come to have no way to get the guidance the neighbors
give a lot of but can barely pronounce the broad efforts
to revitalize the basin the oil in the shed the old lovers
laid a bed behind and didn't take a thing not even a spoon
full of medicine they stare forever now the spruces too

Everything looked different in the dark the daybreak
yawned away from the homestead the hikers couldn't
help from that height the valley looked less exhausted
than the grass fire a good rain galloped over her dead
body she said she wouldn't have it her mind was already
made up about the milking barn new things were being
born besides the branches the birds were on were brittle
now what passed as time was just an outpost that had
a year ago just been the lake is all that's left to do is make
a potion or a master plan she knows the ingredients
are hers to take with her when she goes

A Boy Asks for A Pony

It had come to him in a dream
he had for weeks irregularly
been sleeping with his back turned
to the wall the shadow puppets
purposefully out of mind
the old man made a gesture
toward the acreage his crops covered
up the artifacts buried
under the land he acquired
at an auction years ago
a boy pushed open the bathroom door
where his best friend's older sister bathed
the kittens that were in the box
the builders found a way around
what prevented what they planned
was not the boy the summer brought
to their backyard new blooms
the girls went out and gathered
in the dark the dusk covered cars
wobbled back and forth between
farms the field hands forged
a resistance to the season the dogs
slept through on the porch
a phantasmagoria of moths
a mother lit up like them from inside
the screen came little voices
calling first then yelling for the horse
that cantered all evening around
the cabin they kept their secrets in
a handkerchief a hired hand left

behind the houses on a road
he'd remember later as his own
hands shook with age the boy
got exactly what he asked for
a glass of water to be propped up
to politely watch the dawn
however many hours away it was
cold in the cabin he recalled
the wind had a bite the boat pulled
the water skiers through
it all dad sat up consoling
the kittens the lamplight casted
shadows on the porch perhaps
then it was clear the end
wasn't how it was planned for
or predicted it was just the end

Ergonomics of the Later Land

Everyone in the late age
starts considering longevity.
The lukewarm possibility

of polar caps and the impropriety
of airplane pilots
and their plans. Role-playing

is a thing that happens
there. All the war-torn children
wear whale suits

and wander toward the sea.
In search of some other
calling, the hot-air mechanics

abandon their balloons
and walk away. Whatever worry
winds up in the mind

doesn't matter. The boiling question
is why things begin to break
apart in the first place. The contractor

on duty follows directions
and the project turns out perfectly.
Fine, but to a fault.

According to the levelers the land
        opens and swallows up
the street because it wants to look

        the way we like it. Laughter
is a make-believe medicine made up
        by policy makers whose

prerogative it is to please. *Please*
        is the preferred utterance
of a conspiracist about to continue

        with his speech. Speaking
with some real regard
        to the rendezvous

of weather fronts, the heartland
        is sure to expect
the heaviest of hail. How about that.

        How about the barrage
of snow falling on the mountain top
        a climber rushes to

in an effort to assert her right
        to tell the rest of us
we may someday climb it faster, but

        we cannot climb it first.
Forget what you have heard
        about footsteps. Paths follow

other people's paths and always
        stop at lakes
where perch and trout lie lifeless

        on the shore. All the good
moms tell the bad kids to leave
        the algae blooms alone.

In the grocery store the cashier
        asks the bagger
to get with it. The program

        on the television brings
the populace to tears. Outside the café
        the customers are taken

aback by a stranger's offer to blow
        on their hot beverages.
Innuendo is the language

        of the end. In a bar
the embezzler gets buzzed and coughs
        up an explanation inadmissible

in court. An explosion in the distance
        distracts us long enough
to stop wondering

        what the war criminal
has called for. *I call it like I see it*, says
        the broker who swears she saw

an economy collapsing. No one
        knows where the worker went
or whose responsibility it is now

        to halt the conveyer belt.
It is always a mistake to assume
        the machinery has no mind

of its own. We should have known
        a population on a planet
known for wobbling will wobble

        too. Waking in the wet
sweat of a nervous sleep, a routine
        walker makes his way

toward a routine street. No real purpose.
        No plan to put the barbarous
in their place. Honestly, the people

        had hoped for more space
to feel spectacular. Thought maybe
        they might see

a revolutionary thing. Not representative
        government on the fritz.
Notice now how nothing is

        romantic: no torch
in a steeple, no militiaman in rags
        and on the run. History seems

the safest place and then we remember
how it harms us here.
Making sure the story unfolds linearly

the future is withheld. We have
no idea the ways we will hurt. Having heard
the news has nothing new

to cover, a daughter dozes on
the couch, the decorative pillows
decidedly mundane. When she wakes

she wakes to the sound of the music
box her mother lost, finding it exciting
how suddenly everything stops.

In the Upside-Down Forest of Un-Furious People

In an effort to legitimize a land ethic
the lettuce farmers self-impose a subsidy
on solitude. In certain circles, folks abide
by the fundamental truth: nothing is good
in the world unless the grocery bagger
says it is. For better or worse, management
always mishandles the supermarket
salad bar. Another boy poisons the produce
with a bottle of hair product. The oldest
daughter of the dairy farmer grows tall
and uses a lot of big words, like: *bathymetry*.
It's hard telling what explorers felt, touching
the bottom of the trench. Probably a lot
of pressure. As a people, we're not privy
to the purpose of motion sensors. Make
what you will of the trail-cameras. Someone
loping through the dark neighborhood
turning the dogs on. It's one of those nights
where the moon makes no mention
of itself. A mist creeping slowly
through the soy field. All the country people
putting their faith in the forecast
and placing another log in the fire pit.
On Friday, two people who fought once
in high school will make up at the fish-fry.
This is what commerce looks like
around a lake. Considering the long list of ships
lost on a maiden voyage, the woman
with the new boat goes back and forth
between *Miss Conduct* and *Miss Behavin'*.

We want to see our names all over
everything: the bar, the corner store,
the kids. Had we played our cards right
we might have put it all together: the tarp
covering the crater the airplane left, a man
wearing a tuxedo-t-shirt to meet
his niece, an elderly duo getting busy
building the dog a house that resembles
their own.

The Dark Horse that Directed the Lightning

The storm hit the way
the weather-person said
it would not be like it was
before the barn door
opened outward into wind
the horses emerged
after someone that didn't
understand them said
that they were scared
and startled by the noise
the bats burst forth
from the rafters erratically
and into what
the farm hands felt
they could only describe
as dark and quite unlike
the patterns drawn
out on a document
discolored by the time
the trucks tracked down
the herd the lone horse
in the distance head high
and on its hind
legs the lightning
behind it large and lit up
the landscape stretched on
like the moment
the family the farm raised
woke to find what
they had for so long

called a life was not that
thin wall between two rooms
the youngest
put her fist through
the fence the gate kept shut
every day while growing up
she called to it
and toward her it came
cantering into the hand
with which she held
the fresh oats out
of its mind now or maybe
the farthest into it it's been
the horse raises
up into the dark again
the lightning the truck
lights getting lost inside
the house the prayer
group folds their hands
around the weather
making things unlike
what they were before
the years became
a wilderness their histories
couldn't tame the horse
the hand of oats once fed
upon the flashes
the sky makes at their backs
they bow not in forgiveness
but toward each other
the field between them
like a fathom like a flood

Ideogram of the New Civilian

Everybody claims to be
a new and improved version
        of the introvert. Ask anyone

about the comfort found within
        the absence from the cocktail
party commencing now, just down

        the street. Skeptical of the way
the water smells, the kids hold hands
        and smoke beside

the sewage pond. Little revolutions
        make it hard to disregard
the hours, the character chock-full

        of worry sweating in
the kitchen of what is supposed to convince
        us is a home. I splash my face

like doing so will reinstitute a smile
        and then admire
the floral pattern on the hide-a-bed.

        I hesitate too long and begin
to make myself out in the hallway
        mirror. I say a lot of things

like mischief makes the heart
        grow fonder, or I'm a dream
mechanic, a mad scientist, anything

        really to make myself believe
my motion picture mind isn't a cowboy
        casting existential questions

down a canyon until the echoes
        all come back the same:
as echoes. Notice now the children

        on the rooftops communicating
through their strung-together cans.
        Boredom makes me want

to spill a secret to each bipedal
        organism passing
on the street. I have a heavy heart

        and hope to make amends
with those I've hurt. My hairdresser says
        it sounds like I have some

making up to do so I stop and make
        an angel in the snow.
If I ever get fed up with the weather

        I can, at anytime, pack my things
and leave. I always say I will
        but never really wear a route

into the mountains like a walker
        with a regular routine.
From here they say you can see

        the country, which is a thing
I measure by the cobblestones
        stray dogs callous their paws

upon. I circle around the conversation
        and sensing I haven't said
the thing I came to say, whomever

        I've been speaking to suggests
I quickly cut straight to the heart
        of things. We find the neighbor

face down in the flowers the way
        she always said she hoped
she'd go. Grubs spread fast

        and mortify the lawn. There is
a sunset like there sometimes is, a little
        girl suddenly realizing

when we die we die without knowing
        the next century and how sad
that must be for time. I look for a symbol

        or a sign, not to start or stop, but
to represent the stillness and the constant
        scratching of my head. People sing

and join hands around the crater
in the place where the post office
used to be. A cloud passes through

the froth of factories and we call
forth our breath from the passing
cloud. Each of us, on the inside, gets

a little darker. Like politicians, laws are good
until they no longer are
essential to our governance. It is no surprise

what was sent out
to the black hole did not come back.
For the sake of national security

we ask all the satellites to close
their eyes. It is in this little
blindness that myth mistakes itself

for truth. A child tattles on
another for climbing up a tree
intending never to return

back to the earth. I wipe what I perceive
to be is sweat and seek a place
out of the sun, which leaves these little spots

upon my skin. For my health
I'm told to monitor their hue. This has
everything to do with detriment, but

what is there in all of this: there is a lot
       of sky, a good wind wobbling
the nerves of the orchard workers, a group

       of girls and boys turning
their backs on the far, fading air balloons
       because even wonder wears away.

In the Later Scenes the Setting is Still a Fraud

Every love scene starts
with a pair of lovers
discreet and felicitous
in the corn field
the feeling they felt once
they no longer feel
but are accustomed to
the move the movie
goer makes and duck
their heads what was
not long before your birth
is just I can't recall the word
I'm looking for look at me
twirl to the bathroom and back
in love with the bounty hunter
tipping her hat my way
from the corner booth
how I hate to have to say
for every person feeling good
there are two people
in a restaurant reminiscing
about a friend
that rapidly declined
and what more is there to say
or speak or spread
a blanket out and one around
the shoulders of the someone
a sand dune draws to mind
the air is never what it seems
out there it is exactly like

the midlife hopeful and dirty
like the decades dissolving
behind it and in front
of a small crowd we call
for what we never knew
we needed a concise history
of hazmat suits
a revolutionary's last words
lost to the sunlight
she was executed in
the yard the young boy asks
what everything will be like
after this his mother doesn't say
anything he says he wants whatever
heaven has the house pets
I don't say anything the blue
above us goes on being blue
a car passes and the people in it
pointing at the view
the dust clouds covering
the field the combines part
and come toward us scattering
all that scavenges between
you and me the day
feels like it belongs to us
so we hold it up
and scold it like our own

The Isthmus

It's only the long crossing clouding over.

An uncountable amount of wild.

Now and then the heat making all things less

hospitable. It was history

or all the things that came before it: darkness

and distance and light

from the fire ancient nomads napped beside.

Not to be out done, the sky called

attention to the crater the people pointed

and watched the comet from. There is no

excuse for an echo, no reasonable explanation

something could sound like that

in the canyons. There is only what it means

and whatever meaning they might try

to make of it. At one time there was only the dark

enlarging around us. So long

to solitude and sonar, those otherworldly

nocturnal statutes. So long to the shy

bodies we believed the blue light would liberate.

All the things we vowed to change, changed

without us. It was like mankind and like mankind

it was all unmemorable. It felt important.

To that importance we applied a plaque, the last relic

of our remembering. Seriously, what are we

to make of the landmarks.

*   *   *

It isn't even debatable. The way

we determine if the debut went badly. A shudder

in the flank of a fast beast. A little land

the sea coughed up just enough to cross. First,

for numerous pastures. Then

for the procurement of foreign products. Daily

the debt adds up. There is a horizon

the hungry refuse to head for. Tired of the already

told story, a spy trades his duty for some sleep.

A road. A car on the road we recognize simply

as continuing. Although the quiet could not

know what was coming, it kept calm. All the airdropped

leaflets said the place was liberated. No one knew

what from. The streets were wet and silent and the tired

slept on the slippery bricks. The secret was that

there wasn't one. Just a lot of sky. Not the black one littered

with speck and strata but the everlasting black

behind it. And, of course, a crossing, a strip of land

a shot down pilot swims toward

in the all-consuming alternate, in the cold, in the surrogate sea of hard labor.

*   *   *

The point is that there is no point at which the spear

could have passed cleanly through the coat

the wind wrapped the feathers in. Suddenly everything

built to absorb a blow. A satellite dipping back

through the stratosphere and the land looking dumb

below. Shelters springing up along the strip, though

everyone knew better than to call it safe. A wave. A flash

of light the people wouldn't look toward

because it wouldn't be polite. To point. To speculate

from what end of the spectrum it acquired

all its shine. Radiant and splitting apart

like polar ice, the days pull toward us then melt

away. That old ultimate overabundance of hunger. A sudden

spontaneity of flood. The water already reaching

the roof above the porch the people paddled from.

Somewhere some sense of wonderment, we hope.

A ship going down in the dark. Romantic

from a distance. Starlight. Swimmers synchronized

and surfacing the same. People patting dry

and flagging down what they misperceive

as planes. They didn't think about it. The oil. The rag

a woodworker kept her fingers in. A couple sticks.

For whatever reason the wind wouldn't keep the fire lit.

*   *   *

The weather is exactly what we thought

it'd be: oblivious. Wholly ignorant to its own guarantee

of some great disturbance. Before geography

one could only guess at what bordered and contained

a place. This is the place where everything

happened, all things known and unknown

along this narrow strip of land. It became neither

the scene nor the memory of that scene, stored

in a locket. Water has a short memory, it washes

away all opportunities to make it meaningful.

An acknowledgement. A tacit nod. A transmission

beginning as all said things begin, and, then, arriving

on the other end as static. In this business

of missing there is no happy medium. No synchronized, cross-

code modulation. No membrane thin enough,

no strip of soil that can canal us. There is no short cut

to the incandescent or, more likely, the incandescent

cut short. Whatever is on the other side of that expanding sphere

that contains us has split, has grown long

and in its growing is long gone. It has unzipped the back

of itself and slipped out. When they take inventory

everything is there, but the invisible.

*   *   *

So then lastly the land allows us this: the children

who insist on sprinting through whatever light

is left. All of the parents making their way

out of the water, afraid of what they'll miss. Mostly

antimatter, molecules, and an airplane

moving faster than the sound it makes. Music

and laughter from a ship passing close, but out

of sight. A sound wave on its way back from the end

of space collects things we couldn't possibly

predict. An indefinite ringing, a bell on a boat the foghorn

redirects from harm. All of the land. All of the light

on the routes the travelers refused. And isn't that how

it all goes? Everything gone and a good hat

on the head in a sudden rain. A biker splashing

a puddle upon the two who stop a moment

to embrace. Nobody in their right mind worrying

about the wet. Not one of them finding words

for the bar opening early, allowing them a bite to eat.

How they all stopped and greeted each other

in the street. How the future opened up, drawn out

and long. How the people then were people.

Then nothing. Nothing then, but fog.

NOTES

The epigraph of the book comes from Rachel Carson's *The Sea Around Us*.

"Milankovitch Cycles" refers to the eccentric orbital patterns of planet earth and the effects those cycles have on the climate. The cycles are named after the Serbian geophysicist Milutin Milankovic who theorized their patterning in the 1920s. Much of that poem was inspired and written in awe of Richard Manning's biological history of the heartland: the 1995 book, *Grassland: The History, Biology, Politics, and Promise of the American Prairie*. The epigraph of that poem is taken from a conversation Manning had with the US Fish and Wildlife biologist Pauline Drobney.

The epigraph that accompanies the poem, "These Proliferations," is taken from Louise Glück's poem, "The Sword in the Stone."

"The Isthmus" was written while under the influence of a sun-speckled strip of land along the Stono River, in the West Ashley neighborhood, of Charleston, South Carolina.

This book began in the summer of 2016, on the floor of Nick and Erica Cooper's living room, where I woke one morning to their daughter, Cora, running through the house, running through the light.

ACKNOWLEDGEMENTS

Thanks to the editors of the publications where poems from this manuscript first appeared:

Annulet: a journal of poetry and poetics: "The Waylayer"

Bennington Review: "What if There's Something Out There"

Forklift, Ohio: "Puddle Jumper (p. 32)" and "Puddle Jumper (p. 36)"

Louisiana Literature: "Ergonomics of the Later Land"

Miracle Monocle: "Milankovitch Cycles"

Salamander: "Before the Experts Mislabeled the Beyond" and "In the Upside Down Forest of Un-furious People"

Western Humanities Review: "Puddle Jumper (p. 33)" and "Puddle Jumper (p. 35)"

World Literature Today: "Public Works"

This book owes its heart to the hearts of Mara Rushton, Joyce Rushton, Josh English, and Alana Hatley, the first and only readers of this manuscript in progress.

I bow to Bin Ramke for selecting this book for the Berkshire Prize, giving it its life, and for his exceptional citation.

Thanks to Karla Kelsey, Donna Stonecipher, and Allison Titus. It's a dream and honor to have those three, brilliant individuals interact with my work and offer such generous commentary for the cover.

Thanks to Kristina Marie Darling, Jeffrey Levine, David Rossitter and everyone at Tupelo Press for the time and attention to the book and giving me an opportunity to join the Tupelo family. Thanks to adam b. bohannon for the incredible cover and design.

An immense amount of gratitude to Josh English, my poet partner in crime, without whom this journey would have been a lonesome one. Thanks to him, too, for the many thoughts and ideas on the early versions of this manuscript; for being there every step of the way; for the long conversations that made both my poems and me smarter; and, most importantly, for his friendship.

While few read this manuscript in progress, it was sustained by the inspiration and conversations of many: special thanks to Amanda Mitchell, Dustin Pearson, Peter Twal, and Caylin Capra-Thomas.

Thanks to the inspirational and ordinary interactions of the extraordinary Cassie Davidson, Erica Cooper, Ann and Ryan Olson, Erin Fought, and Matthew Fogarty.

Thanks to Arra Lynn Ross: first poetry teacher and mentor whom, without, I would not be a poet.

Thanks to Samuel Amadon for making my mind think differently about differently thinking and then challenging me to rethink it.

Thanks to Liz Countryman, Ed Madden, Fred Dings, Jim Barilla, and Nikky Finney.

Thanks to everyone at the University of South Carolina who made my time there magnificent and wholly worthwhile. Thanks in particular to everyone there who gave me feedback and support for my poems: Jennifer Bartell, Justin Brouckaert, Melissa Dugan, Daniel Davis-Rogers, Matt Moscato, Betsy Breen, Noah Kucij, Ethan Fogus, Scott Chalupa, Mark Rodehorst, Jennifer Blevins, Anna Barry, Matt

Mossman, Christina Phillips, MC Churchouse, Anton Dela Cruz, and Andrew Valencia.

Thanks to the faculty at Saginaw Valley State University. Thanks especially to the Marshall Fredericks Museum and the fellowship committee for bringing me home as the 2017 Fredericks-Follett-Roethke Research Fellow: Carlos Ramet, Marilyn Wheaton, and C. Vincent Samarco.

Thanks to The Friends of Theodore Roethke and the Roethke Home Museum, especially: Annie Ransford and Mike Kolleth.

Thanks to the English Department at the College of Charleston, especially: Chris Warnick, Scott Peeples, and Myra Seaman.

Thanks to everyone in the Writing Department at Grand Valley State University.

I feel eternal thanks for every single one of my students for their energy, thoughtfulness, and insistence.

An incredible amount of gratitude to Mrs. Stroh, Mrs. Bowen, Mrs. Forystek, Mrs. Vargo, Mrs. Schneider, Mrs. Hillman, and Mrs. Abbott for being the type of teachers' kids in Clio, Michigan needed and still need. Special thanks to Rose Meister, a long-term sub, who once told me to "keep writing even when you don't have to." That encouragement meant so much to my teenage self.

Thanks to the Bates clan: especially Mike, Dawn, Kayla, Cody, and Chase.

Thanks to the Engwall crew: especially Pam, Lorna, Paul, Phil, and Alice.

Thanks to Keith Schneider and Gabrielle Gray.

Thanks to my family: Carl Rushton, Julie Rushton, Lu Anne Hatfield, Morgan Hatfield, Loralei Dunn, Barb, Craig, and Blake Stephen.

Thanks to Josh Arnold, Nick Cooper, Bryan Hughes, and Mike VanAlst—best friends and confidantes, the four most hilariously intelligent individuals I've shared space and time with, whose wit, curiosity, and creativity was formative in the development of my own, and who—these many years—I've had trouble living far away from, but have never lived without.

Thanks to Zach Hatfield, my jazz partner, my soul searcher, my daylight ditty snorter. Thanks for everything, for it all, all those speakable and unspeakable things.

Thanks so much to Mom and Dad for a lifetime of challenges and support, who challenged me to lean in and to push, always, into the further-outs.

Thanks to Juan who watched me from his cat perch and kept me company while I worked on every single one of these poems.

And, lastly, thanks to my partner, Mara Rushton, who makes believing in this life easy, believing in love easier, and whose long-term residence in the light made me want to live there, too.

And, of course, reader, thanks to you.